HOW SHE READ

02 03 04 05 25 24 23 22 21

Caitlin Press Inc.
8100 Alderwood Road,
Halfmoon Bay, BC V0N 1Y1
www.caitlin-press.com

Text and cover design by Vici Johnstone
Cover image: Unknown photographer, portrait of Lorraine Gail Borden, c. 1956. Halifax, Nova Scotia. Writer's collection.
Edited by Canisia Lubrin

Printed in Canada

Caitlin Press Inc. acknowledges financial support from the Government of Canada and the Canada Council for the Arts, and the Province of British Columbia through the British Columbia Arts Council and the Book Publisher's Tax Credit.

Library and Archives Canada Cataloguing in Publication

Gibson, Chantal, author

How she read / Chantal Gibson.

Poems.

ISBN 978-1-987915-96-9 (softcover)

1. Women, Black—Race identity—Canada—Poetry. I. Title.

PS8613.I2945H69 2019   C811'.6   C2018-905969-9

HOW SHE READ

Poems

Chantal Gibson

CAITLIN PRESS

for

Lorraine Gail Gibson
April 7, 1950 – May 8, 1986

Mother loosen my tongue
or adorn me
           with a lighter burden.
                      — *Audre Lorde*

Contents

crossing the punctum

Foreword: How to Use Your Book,
Lesson 1 from *The Coloured Girl's Writing Handbook*

██████████████ Read the story. ██████████████████ look at it carefully ████
████████████████████████████ draw a line ██████ Then write your new words
████████████

— *The Canadian Pupil's Own Vocabulary Speller Text-Workbook Edition, Grade 4,
MacMillan, 1948*

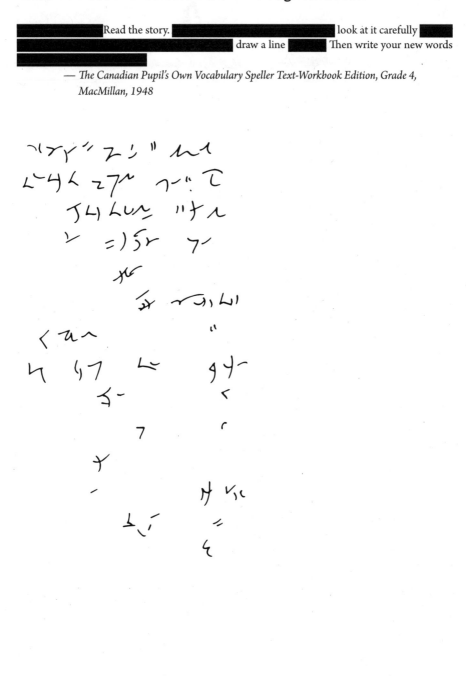

8

How She Read

عربي

Oh, how she read this. Girl
beloved daughter of daughters
blood, kin, and kind

sagacious grammarian
post-fly phoneticist

every syllable she say be sapphires

Oh, how she read that Girl
beloved daughter of daughters
blood, kin, and kind

sassy semiotician
post-def decoder

every book she crack parts oceans,
sends waves rushing back to their shores

every page she turn sets free a caged bird,
whose wings are spread and ready for flight

Oh, how she read, this Girl
beloved daughter of daughters
blood, kin, and kind,

post-dope dissenter
mos-bomb seditionist

every word she speak be a teeth-sucking act of resistance

every word she write be a battle cry

every tap of her pen be the beat of an ancestor's drum

grammar of loss

i've come for your demons

The following list contains words commonly known as spelling demons.
It will be worth your while to test your knowledge of these words.
— *The Pupil's Own Vocabulary Speller, Grade 8, Revised Canadian Edition 1947*

i've come for your demons

      to trouble the lessons

      to enough the letters

      to birthday the disappeared

      to Sunday the boys

      to February the father

      to instead the already

ve'i cmoe fro yuor domens

      to nawodays the conquered

      to awlays the colour

      to aletgethor the women

      to deffernit the samilir

      to freigon the rammarg

      to speratae the stimomees

        from the seruly

Metohr, v'Ie meoc rof oury medons

ot pepole yuor clhotes

ot plestaan ouyr sohe

ot losoe em form het _____ fo Crismhats

proper noun

Some women wait for themselves... and the stars do not care.
— *Audre Lorde*

The North Star?

It didn't fall

ナ) イ' シ !

i dropped it.

missing antecedents

[She] takes ____ in writing correct English, and now she speaks it with the greatest ____.
By paying attention in class she learned to make each pronoun agree with its ____.
In fact she has been very ____ at school.
      — *The Pupil's Own Vocabulary Speller, Grade 8. Revised Canadian Edition, 1947*

                            H_ t_ld h_r m_th_r h_r st_ry

h_d h_l_s _n _t

                            H_ t_ld h_r t_ *st_p!*

m_k_n_g *sh_t* _p

                            H tl_d hr hr stry ws wrttn

n blck nd wht

                            H tld hr th tr_th h_rts smtms

n btwn th bl_ws

                            H tld hr *H* ws *jst*

tryng t tch hr

_ lssn

14

reciprocal pronouns

You i Me

I i You

we i Them

they i Us

We I them

We i each other

we i one another

you i Me

i i you

i i You

you i me

we i them

They i us

we i each Other

                    You i Me
        Them i we   I one another We

      I i You   we i Them
     Me i You   i you I

    they i Us   We I them
   You i I   i me you

  We i each other   we i one another
  Us i they   i us They

  you i Me   i i you
   each other i We   i each Other we

    i i You   you i me
     Me i you   I them we

      we i them   They i us
       You i i   i You i

            we i each Other

You i Me

Them i we   I one another We

i them we   them i We

I i You   we i Them

Me i You   i you I

I Them we   one another i we

they i Us   We I them

You i I   i me you

i Me You   you i I

We i each other   we i one another

Us i they   i us They

i You I   me i you

you i Me   i i you

each other i We   i each Other we

i Us they   us i They

i i You   you i me

Me i you   I them we

I each other We   each Other i we

we i them   They i us

You i i   i You i

i Me you   them i we

we i each Other

dangling modifier

through the world
with
out

hands
n feet all stubs
fumbling

always reaching
for a
light switch

a cruel chain
dangling
in the dark

a tippy toed dint
in the quashed
antecedent

h o l l o w
of her
Christmasslippers

this prosthetic
family
persists

despite
my hapless
limp

misplaced modifiers

She served her daughters
on melamine plates, left

the Royal Albert on the
top shelf waiting for good;

she read them fairy tales
from the Little Golden can-

non of dead mothers in pink
floral head scarfs, trembled

page corners with wet finger-
tips and kissed each one good-

night; she wrote her aubade
at the kitchen table, lit her

smokes on the stove, burned
amber holes in the dark til

every orphanprincess was
Crayola Brown; she stopped

shaking just enough to stay in
the lines, to forge their future,

and set the table for morning.

fragments

for getting grassstains   on my Sundaydress
a life time repenting repeating like   just like
an oil-stained fist likes lemonscented counter-
tops   the way Dixie Cups feared   his widowed

hands lifeline headline heartline   unpaved
potholed   like Grandpa's   black-strap country
logic wrapped twice round a swinging fist full
of misfortune   & the unstoppablemomentum

of grief: like the way he can't stop tracing

your steps the way   I can't stop filling my
pockets with babyteeth   our compulsing past
unfolding a future portended through the lens
of this emptyshotglass like   how I reach for it

another shamemakingnight   & this blank face-
book page so many likes like the scrolling idea
of my happiness too much to bear   such a high
price to pay for a lifetime   repenting repeating

forgetting the grass stains on my Sunday dress

bullet points

— *We Grow Up, The MacMillan Company, 1939*

- P.19 Jupie is a good cat. He lives alone in a little red farm house.

- P. 57 Dick is the mailman on the train. He has bags full of letters and packages.

- P. 62 Jack is a pilot of a big airplane that flies at night. He has a radio.

- P. 88 A brownie is about a foot high. He lives in a cellar. He has a brown face. He looks queer, lives in queer places and does queer things.

- P. 160 Little Ugly Face lives in an old Indian village. She looks so queer that the children laugh and call her Little Ugly Face. She is sad. She has no friends. She really is not pretty at all.

We're all inside watching *Roots* it's January 20 below
another SearscatalogueChristmas packed away in the
attic and you say we just might learn a little somethin
about ourselves about each other these poor raggedy
Africans and the crueltyofwhitefolks how far we've all
come to get here but Nana won't stop tugging the top
button on her brandnewcardigan and Kunta Kinte won't
stop runnin away because he hates his master and his
brandnewname because he misses Omoro&Binta&home
because he never imagined his Africa self in this *toubab*
shutupanddo-as-you're-told land of iron cages collars
shackles and chains so he keeps talkin back and spittin
his Africa name out loud KuntaKinteKuntaKinteKunta-
Kinte like the poisoned tip of an arrow til they hog-tie
his hands and split his back open with a whip tear flesh
from bone til he learns his lesson til he surrenders *it* the
name quiet bloody quivering into ourslackjawlivingroom
and that's when *He* laughs just a little the anvil of his dis-
comfort the mammothweightofwitnessing too much to
bear and we become us and Them wondering was it shame
guilt or ignorance that made *him* say it or centuries of
straightupLaZBoyarmchaircolonialism that made him
say MY NAME IS TOBY in that slow 1970s ABCafter-
schoolspecialretardvoice that's not allowed anymore
theshitnameeverywhitekidwillcallme at lunchnrecess
for months after this godforsaken8dayweek and when
the others laugh too in the wake of our silence I'll pray
KunteKinte will run again no matter what Fiddler says
and when he does get caught—when they take an axe to
his foot—I won't fixate on the screaming I'll remember
KuntaKinte'sdaughterKizzy secretly hocking her nigger-
spit into MissyAnne'swatercup a quick wink of your eye
and therockhardcomfortofyoursmile.

split infinitive

Nope. No proper words back then to rightly
explain how *I* came *to be*. My Webster's and
World Book were as cruel as my Laurentien

Colored Pencils. No dignified labels for the
pigment of my skin, no terms to adequately
mark the historic moment a Black hand and

a White hand could touch each other with-
out somebody going to jail. Now, I live in the half-
life of an epithet. Still, I long to know the *#14*:

Whose lips formed the words *Natural Flesh*?
Whose pen sketched that iconic logo? Who
typeset the snow, sans serifed the font, and

dropped the *u* in colored? Who sold out the
blue dotted Imperial English traced in my 4th
grade speller for the tricks of our neighbors

to the south? Still, I long to touch the bearded,
Xanax-popping Group of Seven holdout wielding
his palate knife, sable brush between his teeth,

painting mountains, lakes, and single trees bent
and twisting in the wind, alone, wasting away in
that snowbound log cabin with the single puff

of chimney smoke—an image I carried daily in
my *Charlie's Angels* backpack and consumed with-
out inquiry. Time has since turned *Natural Flesh*

to *Soft Peach* and *Indian Red* to *Roan*, and I spend
much less of it these days telling Nana not to say
the word mu•lat•to, while I am often reminded

as time shaves lead-filled notions down to the nub,
it leaves behind a splintered rainbow tinder-ready
for a spark, for a torch fueled with the-good-old-

days, for old-timey words *to accidentally reignite*.

homographs

1: a race with skin pigmentation different from the white race (esp. Blacks);

You preferred *coloured* back then, stung less than *negro*. *Mulatto* is dated. I'm *mixed race* now.

2: complexion tint, a characteristic of good health;

No one noticed the colour in your cheeks.
The Christmas dinner one-liner, "Must've been dirty, it even made *you* blush!" At least you taught me how to take a joke.

3: of interest, variety, and intensity;

Remember Cabbagetown? Our coloured beginnings, the dress shop lady, the front door, my broken pointy finger, you in your secretary dress chasing her in the street. *Girl*, where you learn to fight like that?

4: to give a deceptive explanation or excuse for;

The lawyer argued you were coloured by your emotions. Quite naturally, of course. What other reason would you have to beat a white bitch down?

5: to modify or bias;

My world, coloured. Never has a child felt more loved, more protected, more ashamed.

6: an outward or token appearance or form that is deliberately misleading;

You coloured your apology with the single mother story of my one good eye. The white lady dropped the charges.

7: of character, nature;

You said, *Wait long enough, you'll see their true colours.* I never told you she smiled at me as she turned away, or that I stuck my finger in the hinge just to see what would happen.

passive voice

If you can't be free, be a mystery.
         — Rita Dove

She's surprised you're not Jamaican.
Like black flies, you can't keep em off
you.

She's got cousins back east, never been
out that way herself. This bitch can't
find water on a map.

She says you'll find it way colder up here
in the North, like you never seen an atlas,
like you never read a paper, like you never
owned a coat.

She's just being friendly—another teeth-
grinding cliché—she doesn't have to ask
to touch my hair

                    it's just an/Other

                    postcolonialencounter

                         i fear

how you are being, i fear you'll make
a scene, i fear your palm in her face,
i fear how you are being seen by Them,

this jacked mob of 4x4s lined up right
to the back of her mouth, and *I* haven't
started university yet.

There's some shit you know before you
open a book, as visceral as thirst, nausea,   an image
ripe for a stereotype, a gesture awaiting

a minstrelly, toe-tapping soundtrack

                    can you hear it?

Lose it now and they'll forget the Others,
the raghead Indians, the Pakis, the Hindus,
the muck-heads, squaws, bucks, and bush-

niggers, and the only two Fred-Wah-Chinese-
Canadian-restaurant-chinks in town. Mark my
words, they will hyphenate you, find new names

for your gavelled fists. *There's no justice—*

just us.

Show me how to play it safe, Secret Sapphire.
Show me how to smile like Doris Day.
Show me how to say *Have a good one* in your

white lady voice—how to pass on one cliché

for another.

synonyms & antonyms

You *I* her   the East Indian
woman   a black braid twisted
at her waist   a sorry sari   draped snow-
soaked n raggedy   over snow boots   hand em-
broidered cuffs   some other mother's cross
stitch   unspun gold   somebody's yellow longing
for sun   and silk   and sandals

Where did You learn to spurn the golden chirp
of silver bangles? to _____ the marigold of
crimson fingernails?

> (sometimes when
> i'm alone They call me Paki,
> too)

You I them   her children brown
eyes   dark n watery   immigrant brown shit
brown   newcomer brown black hair knotted tight atop
their tiny heads empty spaces broken milk teeth   curried laughter
laughing words strange words stranger words   You can't tell
if they're boys or girls

When did I learn to hold my breath?
>   Onion
>   Ginger
>   Garlic
>   Cumin
>   Turmeric
>   Coriander
>   Some other woman's crushed tomatoes

> (sometimes They ask
> me if i wash my hair
> with buttermilk)

you i Her   Nana
beige cardigan smile   heirloom recipe box   coffee-
stained clippings   blue lined index cards   your first-time fidget-
fingers   simmering water   Wide Mouth Masons   red rubber can-
ning rings   jangling metal lids
large bowl of skinned tomatoes   Her un-
flinching hand   the moment
it touches yours

You I Me
gap-toothed   smiling   already-knowing flinching
was possible

homonyms

You said, *Hand me that knife, girl, handle first.*
I whispered ＼⅄ ⅄＼ into my sorry-looking finger-
nails, prayed you could make Nana's pastry from
scratch, keep that shiny blade away from your skin,
and stop the chemo shakes enough to cut 1 finger

of shortening into 4 cups of flour. We knead our
fingers in a little egg and water to hold it together.
We need our hands to touch and turn this mixing
bowl into a talisman. *Jus skin n bones, girl,* you wink
an elbow into my ribs, pray there's time to make

a woman of me, but you just scratch the surface of
my adolescence. If I'd stop biting my nails, stand up
straight, we wouldn't have to fight tooth n nail to get
along. You play "Stuck on You" for the umpteenth time,
snap your fingers on the downbeat. I count (5, 6, 7,

and 8) every scratch on the vinyl, mutter something
foolish like, *Wish you'd keep your hands off my stuff,*
til your backhand reminds me I am your stuff, always
under your skin, eyes rolling, all sass n backtalk, til
you're itchin to skin me alive. I can't stop counting

down the days til I graduate and nail down a real job.
I'm so full of straight As, you can't praise me or beat me
down. You're too tired to raise a finger and say, *Don't
ever let a man lay a hand on you, girl.* You just ＼⅄ ⅄＼ ,
pass the rolling pin and scratch me off your to do list.

Nana says you damn near scratched the black off, flesh
down to the bone. The white coats took years to nail
down a diagnosis, Hodgkin's, not hysteria, wearing away
your fingertips. When Lionel hit No. 1, you didn't have
a prayer. Nor did I really, an unfinished woman, stuck

on you, praying for second chances, a white-knuckled
life, the surface slightly scratched. I remember to untuck
my thumbs to avoid snapping my fingers whenever I get
the nerve to throw a punch. The white coat says I'll be fine.
If you were here, would you paint my nails or nurse me

with the back of your hand?

faulty parallelism

a stick

a stick of chalk

ナ イ ゛ニ

Nana tracing tickle letters on my back

a jack pine

a jackknife

a North Star

the North Star

a freshly sharpened HB pencil

a storybook

A September Gale

your MacMillan Grade 4 speller

a maple key

a snowflake

that tiny flake of scalp on your afro pick

a black wench

a black hole

a backhand

a bloody nose

the difference between an Indian

and a Chinese sunburn

subordinate clause

because you were my first book
because yours was my first face

because your first look was sorrow
because your second was love

because I charted your scalp like an atlas
sectioned your hair to the roots with the pointy tip
of a tail comb, discovered your pink secret
at the crown, and released the ancestral sighs
of fingertips and VO5

because I studied the slight coffee stain
on your side teeth right next to the fake one
in the front and the soft constellation of tiny
black moles on the rise of your right cheek
every time you smile

because I memorized the monthly swell of your
breasts and the water bloat of your ring
fingers, because I feared the dark potholed alleys
of your palms and the black slap of Jesus sandal
against my thigh

because *she* was your first book
because hers was your first face

because your first look was sorrow
because her first look was shame

because they called you ugly
because I am your spitting image

(because there are no honest poems
about dead women)

because I wrote every line twisted
in the furrow of your brow

...if I say in this letter, I'm waiting
to step into another life,
will you come then and find me?
— *Dionne Brand*

icons

c words

How do you tell the trope-
weary c _ r _ t _ r?

> The c _ nt _ nt's not old,
> —it's c _ nt _ n _ _ _ s.

> I c _ n't help trippin
> over c _ l _ _ r _ d girls.

How do you c _ nv _ y it
yet again?

> I'm not
> picking
> at the wound,

> i'm just
> trying
> to c _ _ t _ r _ z _ it.

How do you c _ nfr _ nt the past
with a c _ l _ n _ z _ d tongue?

> Truth is.

> I c _ n't.

An Introduction to Cultural Studies (for EJ)

You used to sit with me while I'd take a bath, til
you were about eleven, chat and count the Avon
bath beads you gave me for Christmas. I doubt
it ever occurred to you that a woman with three
kids might want a little time alone. For a while,

you'd always bring some book or magazine,
Judy Bloom, Nancy Drew, some *Teen Beat*,
Tiger Beat foolishness with white boys on it,
the *Toronto Star*, the Sears catalogue, a *World
Book Encyclopedia*—but, you wouldn't read

them to me, you'd just tell me about what you'd
learned, if you liked them or not—always white
pieces of blue-lined three-ring binder paper torn
and placed between the pages you prepared to
discuss. When you preferred that Shaun Cassidy

over his brother, David, I asked what coloured
boys did you like, but you couldn't think of any,
except for Michael Jackson. But you didn't like
him in *that way*. When the Beatles invaded in
'64, I didn't like Sam Cooke in that way, either.

I remember '77, the summer of Emanuel Jaques,
The Shoeshine Boy found dead on a rooftop in a
garbage bag. I nearly wept when you asked me
about Yonge St., faggots, body rubs, as if I'd know
how those child raping degenerates could drown

a young boy in a sink. You Scotch-taped the *Star*
clippings in saran wrap, careful to keep them dry.
When you said, *Mom, only poor kids get lured away
and snatched in bags,* I understood your insistence
and stopped reading your sisters *Curious George.*

Sometimes, I'd watch you watching me, your gaze:
water beads in my fro, my big boobs floating in the
fake-lavender-scented water, my pink C-section scar,
the wiry hair between my legs, like you were trying
to figure me out, like you were trying to see the future.

Close Reading: The Black Wench Suite

1. black holes (or how to form a stereotype)

Miss Dinah preferred the Cape of Good Hope; but she was afraid of *the Caffres*, who sometimes carry off white women. To elope with a lord or a duke, she observed, would be a very pretty incident: but, should any person ever write a novel about the Gosling family, to be carried off by *a Hottentot*, would appear so droll.
　　　— *Thomas McCulloch*

Lookit. Most words are harmless if you
just let them be. Others can be downright
n _ sty, like bl _ ck h_les—their pull savage

enough to wrest fact from fiction, to suck
science from satire, enough to convert
a small Puritan Nova Scotia town into

a Parisian theatre at the Palais-Royal.
A proper noun may contain the missing
link between animals & humans, a name-

less black woman, more n_ked than nude,
the Hottentot Venus, a n_ppy-h_ _ d_d h_
shaking her t_ts and her big bl_ck _ss

inside an iron cage, the specimen Sarah
Baartman spreading her _frica legs wide
for the New World, tw_rkin her fr_ _ k-

show lady parts, her anatomy destined
for glass jars of formaldehyde, once the
smallpox has done its work, while ladies

& gentlemen come, with proclivities and
charcoal sticks, feather pens and fetishes,
scales and scalpels, kinks and charms,

methodologies and microscopes, searching
for the reason behind the races,

　　　　　　　　squeezing　—
　　　　　　　　all that matter
　　　　　　　　into such a tiny
　　　　　　　　space,

s_cking
th_ l_ght
fr_m a
d_ing
st_r.

2. First Encounter with The Thing

From the beginning I found one question insisting itself: when precisely did the author
know she was in trouble?
— *Toni Morrison*

Africa, West Indies, America, which dank
ship brought her here?

p5:   she's the black wench in a house
        of new-money white folks, your Mr. & Mrs.
        Gosling & their parasoling daughters

        a maid who can't make a meat loaf

        a black spot in your New World

Slave, indentured, freeborn, Loyalist, can You
tell me where she's from?

And what does she look like to You?

        distinctive man, author, intellectual, teacher,
        first principal of Dalhousie, mentor to future
        university presidents, man of distinction,

        some archetypal Aunt Jemima?
        some Georgian Mrs. Butterworth?
        some antebellum Florence Johnston?

or

some sorry southern white girl's
Hollywood movie mammy?

What ahistorical source birthed her representation?

p6:   she's in the kitchen flat on her ass, arms
         n legs splayed out on the floor, a fallen star,
         a sopping snow angel, apathetic kitchen savage
         wrestling *Mammoth*, Gosling's giant boar

Tell me, how did Mammoth the pig get *his* name?

We're discussing You and the early tradition of
Canadian satire. i'd like to raise my hand to ask
a question, just like I did in Grade One:

> so strange her being here, Him placing her
> at the start, the Caffres, the Hottentots,
> the fearful white women, such a big black
>
> _____, so much darkness packed in this tiny world
> of white folks falling,
>
> > losing touch with God,
> >
> > > with the land,
>
> call it satire,
> > > i get it, it's just
>
> He gave Gosling a past, a present, a family,
> and a New World to fuck up in, meanwhile
>
> He left her _____ writhing on his floor.

Tell me, *how* do i begin to untangle centuries of _____,
to extract the shit in the text from the shit in Your head

before we move on to Leacock?

> (but, *I can't move on* this book this class this room
> is a minefield truth be told i won't put my hand up
> i won't say a word because i'm scared so fucking
> scared i'm wrong thinking these thoughts because
> she's really just a secondary character because it's
> very impolite to disrupt this lecture because i'm the
> only brown girl here and i haven't read Toni Morri-
> son yet because AmLit isn't til spring and *I* won't
> meet Fanon, Lorde, & Brand til grad school because
>
> > *I* feel light-

headed from knowing something discovering some-
thing true and dangerous for the first time some-
Thing about a mailman named Dick and a pilot with
a radio named Jack Brown and a queer brownie that
lives in a cellar in a coal basket that leaves black marks
on white tablecloths and brown-little-ugly-faces with
no friends and tiny-naked-Africa-people with no words
and the tips of poisoned arrows and the numb throat-
swelling effect of tasting a shiny red fruit for the very
first time in the presence of my slack-jawed classmates
and thinking somebody's gonna call me a racist or say
some shit about reverse racism whateverthefuckthatis
and because i'm the crazy one because I'm privileged to
be here because I should be grateful because there are
way worse places to live because I should just leave if
i don't like it here if i can't say anything nice because
i know I am in trouble feeling feeling emotional feeling
maybe a little tragic even just thinking her only home
was his imagination)

What was the narrative moment, the specular even spectacular scene that convinced her she
was in danger of collapse?

p119:   so, I keep reading, turning pages to see
          if You give her a line, a tiny sound, a cry,
          an utterance, a sign that tells me *You* know

          she's human, but when I meet her brother
          near the end, after the fox trap, when I find
          out he's not really *the devil*, just a shadow,

          a silhouette in a moonlit window seen through
          the drunken lens of the town's finest, i wonder,

          Ddue meoc no onw, wath het fcuk?
          Waht indk fo impsteriali bllusits si hist?
          Hist si waht calturul meghemyon lokos ikle!

Tell me, what weighty price would *You* have paid for
giving her a name?

3. 'Nuff Said (after Nina Simone)

I ain't got

        no land
        no home
        no people
        no God
        no story
        no man
        no bed

but

        I got heels
        cuz these crazy white folks always nippin

        I got sense
        cuz these Gosling bitches always trippin

        I got a tongue
        for keepin secrets and another one for tellin

        I got one ear
        trained on gossip and the other one on yellin

        I got my eye
        on the youngins
        watchin out for men with treacherin hands

and at night,

        I got these arms
        around my woman
        when we're makin love (and makin plans)

Portrait by Harvey B. Lindsley, *Harriet Tubman, full-length portrait, standing with hands on back of a chair*, c. 1871–1876. Library of Congress Prints and Photographs Division Washington, D.C. 20540 USA http://hdl.loc.gov/loc.pnp/pp.print, LOT 5910.

Don't Call Me Minty: A Revisionist Heritage Minute

Tubman later realized that the only way to she could gain her freedom was to run away. *She did follow someone who was making his way to freedom, only to suffer a serious head injury.* Despite suffering from seizures and sleep attacks brought on by the injury, Minty later married John Tubman, a free Black man.
— *Historica Canada*

)¬⅂⌐\\! *Listen.*

I did *not* follow someone
  I was in a dry goods store with a plantation cook
  buying items for the house

I did not follow Barrett's slave,
  the someone in the store who left his plantation work
  without permission

I did not follow Barrett's overseer,
  the someone in the store who ordered me to help him tie up
  the slave who got away

      They call it TLE, temporal lobe epilepsy, look
      it up, the injury the overseer, the missing some-
      one, brought down on me directly with an
      object intended for the slave who got away.

      He cracked open my skull, drove my mistress'
      scarf deep into my head. Someone carried me
      fainting, laid me down on the seat of a loom.
      I remember wiping bloodnsweat from my eyes.

Despite my suffering?

                    seizuresnsleepattacks
                    anxietynaphasia
                    visionsndysphoria
                    aurasnamnesia .

I survived my assailant.

Despite my suffering?
              I remain

43

your #North Star
your #Freedom Seeker
your #Black Lady Moses

You should have named him.

When it comes to freedom) ᛝ ᚾ ᛝ\ I'd rather take
my somnambulant chances stumbling stark naked
and alone in the open through the lynchy day-
light backwoods of Maryland with a tiny quail
feather for a compass than stand *here* posed, lace-
necked by the blunt savagery of your prose.

Call it an oversight, a page constraint
—but don't call me Minty. Pet names
are meant for friends and lovers.

Call it shoddy, call it systemic, two dark
paths, one happy ending. Either way,
You meant no insult, no injury, I'm sure,

yet, either way) ᛝ ᚾ ᛝ\ I do not follow.

Centrefolds: Delia & Marie-Thérèse on Opening Night

she took care not to lose the signs
to write in those eyes what her fingers could not script
— *Dionne Brand*

Hey, Girl. What's your name?

Africa.

Who did that to you, Africa?

Science.

Science? Hm. Cruel piece of work.

Objective.

Wha?

It's Objective.

Objective my ↑ ⌐ ⅄ !
Nothin ob-jec-tive about wrestlin
that sorry dress round your waist.
What kind of Science leaves you
with your lady parts hanging out?
What kind of animal does that?

He believes I am the animal.

What? What the?

I am his Evidence.

↑ ⌐ ⅄. Come on now. Evidence?
Is that what He call you?

I'm intended for textbooks, micro-
scopes, and lecture halls, not art
galleries and museum walls.

Girl, please. Evidence of what?

Our place. Our inferiority.

Our?

45

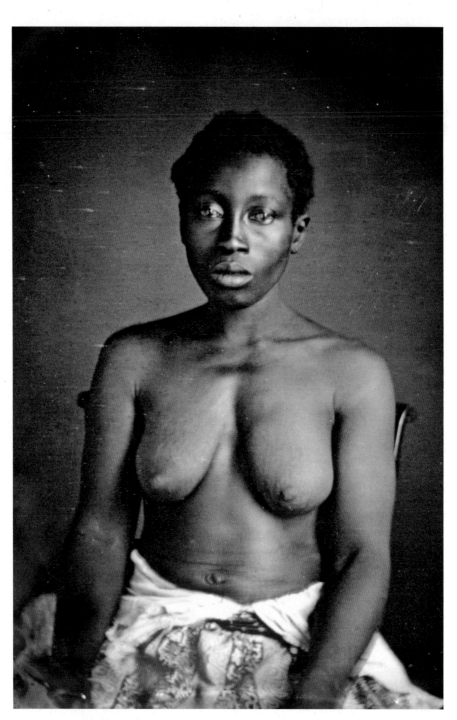

Portrait by Joseph T. Zealy, Daguerreotype, Delia, frontal, c. 1850. Delia, Country Born of African Parents, Daughter of Renty, Congo. Courtesy of the Peabody Museum of Archaeology and Ethnology, Harvard University, PM#35-5-1/053040.

Painting by François Malépart de Beaucourt, Portrait of a Haitian woman, 1786. McCord Museum, M12067.

Our. Up *here*, we're the same,
just different.

You're right. You ARE evidence.
Evidence of how messed-up-
in-the-head He is! Science is
a trip. He used you, Girl.

Different time. Different frame.
I remain a black woman with
her breasts on display.

Hm. I hear you. Just look at em
lookin at us, readin the captions,
disclaimers, trigger warnings,
hidin behind their cellphones,
tryin not to stare.

Trying not to get caught.

That's right, Girl. You know,
they're here to see these. *Nasty.*

And who did *that* to you?

Art.

Also cruel.

Yep. Just look at em. One
poppin out of my top, the other
pokin out of my armpit. Nipples
like bullets. Fucking amateur.

And his argument?

Aesthetic.

You're kidding.

Nope. You're naked. I'm nude.
Same, but different.

But, you're so—

Com-posed?

Yes. Composed.

ㄴ ㄴy ⌒ !

And the fruit?

Evidence.

Of?

That this mo'fucker can't paint for shit.

I can't tell which one is worse,
the photograph or the painting.

Seriously? The painting, hands down!

I'm not convinced.

*Look here. You'll find me in every
Canadian art history textbook and
no one talks about how badly I'm
drawn, how poorly I'm rendered.
I know Realism hadn't kicked in
yet—but come on now.*

*At least you look like you, a woman,
your skin, your arms, your stomach,
your breasts, your neck, your mouth,
your nose, your eyes, your beautiful sad,
sad eyes. You look like somebody's child,
somebody's daughter, somebody's sister,
somebody's lover, somebody's friend.*

*Somebody can see you, if they're brave
enough to look. Girl, you pretty, just like
that shiny Sister on the front cover of*
The Book of Negroes.

The medium?

Nope. The message.

And you?

*Girl, I'm a straight-up bad representation.
A material image of a white man's idea of*

a black woman who posed for a portrait
with a pineapple.

Hm. Simulacra.

Mm hmm.

Then why are you *here*?

Here? Listen, I may not look real, but I am
one of a kind—a West Indian domestic
slave in 18ᵗʰ century New France, I AM
EVIDENCE. I am history, Sister! I'm a
historic Sister, a fine Black woman in a
white Canadian landscape; a slave
where slaves ain't supposed to exist.

So, you disrupt the freedom myth.

Girl, I tear that shit up.

But there are so many myths, tropes, types.

Tell me about it. Mystify n simplify. Mystify n
simplify. Disrupt one, perpetuate another.

The pineapple?

The god-damned-pine-ap-ple, the head-scarf,
the neck-lace, the boob, the blouse, the pose,
the smile. I'm straight-up property, here for
the white male gaze: an exotic import, touch
with your eyes, not with your hands!

We're invisible, yet draped in clichés.

Yep. Same but different. Still stereo—

Wait! Ssh! Did you just hear that?

You mean, "At least they weren't down
South picking cotton"?

"Could have been worse"?!
Ya, I heard it. You'll get used to that.
White folks up here got a thing about us

singin n pickin cotton. *They* write songs
n plays about that shit.

"At least"? *'₹ ⱶ* What does that mean?
What about here? What about now?
Hey, Dumbass! Can't you read?

That's it, go on.

It says A-fri-ca-via-South-Ca-ro-li-na!

That's it. Get it out.

It's called CON-TEXT. GET SOME!

Alright now. Calm down. He can't hear you.
He ain't listenin. Call it guilt, ignorance,
arrogance, or straight-up stupid—it's just
another microaggression.

A micro what?

Microaggression. That's the new word
for the seemingly little ways They fuck
with us every day. Insult here, snub there,
joke-joke, my bad, just kidding—wha?

Art?

Yes, Science.

 I have to do something.

Now, now. Don't go gettin

—hysterical? I have to *do* something.

What, Girl? What you gonna do?

)ⱶ⸍⸝

What?

Smile.

What!!

51

I'm. Am. Going. To. Smile.

Seriously?

Yep.

But you supposed to be objective.

Supposed to be.

But you gonna mess with time n space n shit! You're being—

Unreasonable?

They're just gonna reclassify you.

So?

Call you by another name.

So?

So? So, which one you gonna do? The Sapphire, the Jezebel, the Mamm—

The Mona.

The Mona? Woman, have you lost your mind?!

Perhaps.

But that's Ap•pro•pri•a•tion!

Yep.

Mad evil, your calculatin. Now, let's get this sorry selfie-takin son of a bitch right here.

Long beard, short pants?

Yep. Jus wait. Jus wait'l he turns around, til he's focused, til he's centred, til he's lost in his own reflection.

Excerpts: Marie-Joseph Angélique, Montreal 1734 (for Afua Cooper)

The stars will fall. The sun will cease
to shine. Light will collapse in on itself. ...
Darkness will resume her peaceful reign.
      — *Lorena Gale*

I told them I did it.
I told them I did it with
a small stove. My choice, a decision fuelled
by reason.
Unlike the Court, neither
mob nor man influenced my hand. Folks
here say I am capable and culpable of bad
thoughts. It takes just one
to burn down a city. I swear to God
I told the truth, just not the one
the King's Law required. Yes, my confession

Break vb
:to fracture

broke *after* the hammer, marrow spurting
from my bones, yet my screams proved
unconvincing. How could I act
alone, *sozinho*, without
an accomplice? Justice desired
my white lover's name. Just a whisper,
an utterance, some small
sign of him, might have saved me
from the match.

They believed I'd break before the first swing.

:to separate into
parts with suddenness
or violence

Ask any woman who's given birth to ghosts
—I was already broken.

One gave me bread, the Other, babies.
Love takes many forms.

The indentured servant to my mistress
prepared our shelter, hid loaves in a barn across the
river at Longueuil. Together, we waited for the ice to
set; we got as far as Chambly.

53

The slave from Madagascar, his master
a friend, an associate of my own. Go ahead,
infer us together, just another business
arrangement, or conjure our embracing,
black bodies lit by candlelight, torched
silhouettes writhing, inflamed
with the romance of empire.
Eustache lived for one month.
Louis, two days.
Marie-Françoise, five months. A blessing
:to render inoperable   none of them lived
long enough
to call
me
Mãe.

First name *Filha*, last *Incendiare*.
One whispered at my birth, the other embroidered &
emblazoned on my chest.
There have been others in-between. This one
:to interrupt, suspend   is common, so don't overthink it.
It turned Protestant to Catholic, heathen to believer. I
was baptized in the Code Noir.
My mistress couldn't break
with tradition. Once, she birthed a
daughter, named her Marie Angélique.
Again, resist the savage pull to search for
sentiment in my name. You'll not find
love in the dark. She sold me for a barrel
of gunpowder. If this tiny detail ignites
an interest in history, if you find yourself
here in Old Montreal, filling *in the gaps*
between the churches, cafes, & condominiums...

and I've known the intimacy of women,
a mother's breast, a sister's hands
braiding my hair with the whispers of
ancestors, the sister scholars combing my charred
remains, literally parting fact from
fiction, excavating me from the myths,
an aggravating sisterhood, an eye-rolling,
teeth-sucking mob, stitching together
a life in pieces. Feel their hands placing
me at the centre; feel the tremor in
the landscape.

:to make or show discoveries

If you *still* find yourself wanting, filling in
the holes, re-lacing the boots, tightening
the screws, inserting the wooden wedge between my
knees, imagining what's
underneath my shift—STOP. *Stop it!*
and ask yourself, Why? Why so
much time is given to what's
been done *with* my body,
with our bodies.

Now, ask me what I want done *to* my body.

:to alter sharply in tone,
pitch, or intensity

my daughter? the tiny rise and fall of her chest,
every inhale, a cooing, hand-clenching, foot-
kicking act of resistance, the gravity of her
first smile
a haunting little fragment
enough to make me a little crazy.

:to begin construction

Sad Young Black Girl Perched on Bench, c. 1870–1880. Tintype. Richard Bell Family Fonds, Brock University Archives, James A. Gibson Library, http://hdl.handle.net/10464/3637.

Wanted: Sad Young Black Girl Perched on a Bench, 1870–1880

Mama says, Ƴ (-) ᐳ ! *Girl, why you gotta look so*
miserable? Look at me, propped up on this bench,
sad trees behind me—nobody's woods should look
like this. This Sundaydress feels like jail. Achinarms,
squishtoes, picture takin ain't nothin to smile about.
Wish I could rip this bow from my neck and unloosen
Mama's grip on these laces, but she wants you to know
we got a little money.

Mama says, *Nothing good can come from a girl*
wearing pants (unless you're playin Underground
Railroad). Deep inside my coat pocket, you'll find
my compass, my jackknife, and a map with an x
for every oak, pine, and maple with my mark on it.

Mama says, *Girl, you got too much imagination,*
the way you carry on in those woods! She says
somebody's gonna see me playin in those trees,
talkin to myself, lookin crazy with all my day-
dreaming. Deep down, she's scared somebody's
gonna think I'm up to no good, somebody with a gun,
a sack, and too many hands. When she catches me
smiling, she winks and says, *Should I call you simple or*
sly? Then she laughs like syrup when I Ƴ (-) ᐳ and say,
You should call me Minty.

Mountain Pine Beetle Suite

I. dendroctonus ponderosae

They come with axes between their teeth. Pioneer beetles,
females hungry for trees, ready to carve an instant town   out

of the wilderness. Somewhere in the needling green sprawl
between Darwin & God, an edict etched deep & tingling

beneath the skin, they believe *this* stand of old pines will last
a lifetime. By nature, they desire. A species wants

nothing more than to procreate. Back home,
a pheromone frenzy stirs a gnashing appetite

for industry. The new believers wake & uncross
their legs, hell-bent on leaving this unholy land

of hollow trees. How soon they forget the splinter's prick
between their lips. In unison, they hum, the blue-

stained settlers, young males itching to leave this once-
Eden girdled & snap-necked. A ghost town rusting, their dead

pitched out of the trees. Meanwhile the humans look
petrified, like butterflies shocked in resin, arms wide,

palms flat against the front room window, disbelieving
the *FOR SALE* sign on the lawn, wishing away

the dust on the toys piled up in the driveway.

II. summer: mating season

the female plays house   between
the bark & the sapwood   she is
hard-wired for love   in the phloem
her scent on the walls   she rubs
her Avon wrists together   & waits

the male finds her intoxicated they
make love under the trees legs be-
come arms hands grow fingers nails
scratch   tiny love notes   in the bark

summer is short here   little time
for courtship in the North: the cold-
blooded retreat to the woods veins
pumped with antifreeze the female
bores deeper into the sapwood she
drags her smokes & her big belly up
the tree carves her birthing chamber
and her coffin with her teeth

III. homo sapiens

Girl, there's a red stain on your floral dress
trying hard to look like a rose. Usually

you don't bleed this much.
It just takes a minute to stop:

a dab of Vaseline, a greasy piece
of rolled up toilet paper shoved up

your nose, the tissue bent
and twisted a few times

to reach the broken blood vessels.
In the back of your mind, you know

you'll have to see the doc, probably
have it cauterized. Tell him it was just

an accident, no need to fill out a report (no
big deal). It's a small town, after all.

Everyone talks. But no one told you
it would look like this, marriage:

your high school sweetheart, a sawmill job,
a house, two kids, a camper, a truck,

and a severance check.
You borrowed

your mother's fairy tale, a ponytail dream
you can get with a Grade 12 diploma.

It all started with a forest and a knife
and an old pine tree with your name on it.

Remember? The hands
that lit your smokes first,

that wooed the knot from your halter top
and filled the back pockets of your jeans,

that drew circles on your round belly
and caressed your pink baby scar,

have somehow forgotten
how to touch you without leaving

a mark. A little foundation and some lipstick,
and you're good as new, right? Tell the kids

you'll be out in a sec. It's time
to get ready for bed. Tuck in

your pocket an extra white tissue, just in case
the bleeding starts. *Daddy will be back soon*

to tell you a story. Is that what you'll say—
this time—when you open the bathroom door

and try to smile away the swelling, when you find
a kitchen chair in front of the fridge, and your 4-year-old

daughter holding out a bag of frozen peas?

IV. obituary

wide mouth masons, shard glass, steamed
cabbage, boiling water n beets, some days
her countertops wept and the white tile floor
was a blistering purple sea

let us remember the curved lines bracketing her
parenthetical smile

sometimes she missed the 401 exit to _____ Street
and followed the broken line to Guysborough bi-
secting her fists, not long before the beetles came
and the old pines laid down their weary branches

she surrendered to Science: a needle-punctured
landscape, pretending Prince George had a coast-
line, she traded the shit stank of pulp for the scent
of Atlantic sea salt

she was a card reader, a fortune teller, a knocked-
over stop sign that said, *No one promised you a life
without corners*

she taught her daughter how to make a fist, to un-
tuck the thumb, expose it just enough to take the
impact of a punch without breaking

she giggled when he called it *croshit*, after she took
to crocheting afghans and doilies, nothing prepared
him for a widower's life of small cups of soup & half
sandwiches

she leaves behind a question mark, a flickering
light, and a northern village of bones, a peaceful scene
staged on a lake in the quiet corner of morning, as if

she has every intention
of coming back

crossing the punctum

-)ᴡᴧ)

The Tiny People: How to Use Your Book

I know your discoveries are most important—to you, to the nation, to God, and our Queen, but what of me, David? Why is silence my lot?
— *M. NourbeSe Philip*

See Your Words.

The Tiny People

Smaller than any other race in the world in Africa. They wear very little clothing.

only a child.

no language of their own.

a poison that kills anything it touches.

Know Your Words.

smaller than any other race in the world

They are here somewhere in all of this

in Africa they wear very little clothing

I can tell you the English lost, that Wolfe
died a hero on the Plains of Abraham. I
can deconstruct Benjamin West's Neo-
classicism, colour, composition, content.
I can theorize the Other, the Indian,
the Nobel Savage kneeling at his feet.

only a child no language of their own

—yet, i cannot speak of my ancestors?

a poison that kills anything it touches

My silence is a sentence.

Study Your Words.

Write Your Words

Hegemony. He·gem·o·ny.
Hegemony gets me down.
He gets me down.
He gets me down.
He gets me down.

Editorial: A Letter to the Sisters of Society

It was not only the white antislavery establishment that held her at arm's length; she also perceived that black women were uncomfortable with her visibility as a publisher and an activist.
— *Jane Rhodes*

Mary Ann Shadd, The Provincial Freeman, October 21, 1854

What is it about us that furls our fingers into fists,
hands clenched, white knuckled with the fear
of being seen?

Who taught you to see poverty in the mirror? To crack
under the pressure of your own tiny reflection?

Use my ~~light~~ skin, my class, my education, call me
uppity
behind my back

Can't you see?

Your disdain for me is just
a distraction.

What is it about us that furls our fingers into fists,
white knuckled with the fear of being seen choosing
a side?

Who taught you to stand at the back of the line?

Use my ~~big~~ words, my press, my occupation, call me
Ms High n Mighty
behind my back

Don't you know?

The first link in an iron chain was once
the last.

What is it about us that furls our fingers into fists?
White knuckles clenched over your head? His fear
of seeing you choosing a side?

Who taught you to edit your tongue?
To redact your thoughts?
To retract your feelings?

Use my voice, my stance, my fisted pen, call me
crazy ~~bitch~~
behind my back

Don't you know?

He can't touch you now
without your consent.

Sisters of society, what is *it* about us standing *here*
nowtogethersidebysidemattering arms raised up
over our heads, fists clenched punching the sky?

It's not our fear of him. I mean, which one of us is left
unmarked? What tiny hole remains untaken?

It's knowing *we* are enough. Our fear *is* Him ~~not~~

seeing us choosing

       a side

       a stance

       each other.

Unknown photographer, c. 1967. Image of CPR Mixed Bowling Team, Halifax, Nova Scotia. Writer's collection.

Mixed Bowling

1.

'74, I came home from Miss Neering's
Grade One-Two split, in the classroom with

the orange, scratchy carpet that hated my
stockinged feet with sparks, where I sat up

straight in the front row, Queen Elizabeth
looking down, standing hands-cupped on

a velvet chair, blue sash n sapphires, smiling
like Nana, where I learned to raise my hand

before speaking. I wasn't sure, when I burst
through the front door, if the *bow-tied Black*

man in the black & white photo on my night-
stand was really sitting in our living room.

His Halifax laugh was too big for our Durham
County windows. They shook every time

he clapped his hands. His feet dangled over the
arm rest, pink side up, when he slept on our

polyester couch. He was dark and shiny like the
telephone. I could only see the whites of his eyes

and teeth, when he caught me nosy-parker-in-the-
night, tippy-toeing for a closer look. He looked real

happy to see me. He said, *You know, you've got
school in the morning, girl,* as he reached for it,

the pomegranate, a shiny, scarlet secret next
to the plastic bag of Co-op apples in the fridge,

and when I asked, *What's that?* he placed it in my
upturned palm and said, *You're about to find out.*

2.

second year, Art of the Renaissance, the Bosch
will fuck you up

no one seems to notice in all the groping and ass-
fucking the little Black girl looking out from the centre
panel, a red fruit atop her head, another in her hand

you'll lie, tell your friends Jacob Lawrence is your
favourite painter

different time, different Renaissance

3.

ancestor, showed up silk-tied and cuff-linked,

to Nat King Cole you round the floor
to Cha-Cha-Cha Aunt Ethel til her shoe broke
to laugh when drunk Shirley licked icing off his face
to last-dance me to Puppy Love

before his heart stopped

one week

after the pomegranate.

4.

Do you think mixed refers to gender?

That's what your advisor will ask
when you're contextualizing the photo

66 C.P.R. 67
MIXE
NG

while you're searching for your Nova Scotian
ancestors, two years after the black wench.

like i said:

the North Star

I dropped it

5.

... and when you're sitting in the Prado 20 years
later, in front of *The Garden of Earthly Delights*,
taking in the madness of the centre panel, and
you see the carbon black female figures in the fore-

ground, flat, silhouettes bearing shiny red fruit
atop their tiny heads, the young girl in the bottom
left corner, looking out beyond the frame, away
from the savagery behind her, hiding a tiny piece

in her hand behind her back—you can let it go,
the bitterness—you're *Here*, you made it, no more
surprises, five centuries after the first brush stroke.
You will never know your ancestors, but you will

come to love this masterpiece and the little Black girl
whose one-time grandfather has just come to visit.

Simcoe Days

I had my first crush in Grade 4.
I was in love with a boy. I think

his name was Kelly. A Grade 6
crossing guard, he looked a lot

like Shaun Cassidy, Joe from ABC's
The Hardy Boys. White boy, blond

hair, fringed Indian jacket, arms
out straight, he looked both ways

up and down Simcoe St., the city's
scoliotic spine named for a white

man, who couldn't stop Chloe Cooley
from being sold across the Niagara,

like a nasty yard-sale couch.

——

This morning she says, *Get up, girl!*
reminds me again, *It ain't just a*

Roots thing. Coloured kids couldn't
sleep in late, let alone go to school

back in Simcoe Days, not even the
light skinned ones like me, like Kizzy

couldn't learn to read and write
til Missy Anne whispered ABC,

winked and hushed a stick in her
hand. And look what happened:

Kizzy forged Noah's travelling pass,
Anne turned Judas, and Bell n Kunta,

cried, *We told you, girl!* Kizzy got
sold, tossed in a wagon, ass over

teakettle, spit-kicking all the way to
her master's house, and had a mulatto

rape baby named George.

—

I stood at the crosswalk, scratchy wool
scarf twice wrapped around my face,

pretending my mother's dark silhouette
away from the window, our tiny house

squatting next to a convenience store.
I prayed she wouldn't eye me eyeing

Kelly, an Eskimo hood zipped over
his face. I imagined him smiling at me,

wondered if he watched *The Hardy Boys*
last night at seven or *Roots* at nine.

I didn't ask, I just watched his hands,
one, a shiny red octagon, the other,

five gloved fingers and an out-turned
palm, so, I stopped— and waited for

the red light to turn green.

—

On a fringe-jacket day, at recess,
Kelly waved me behind the oak tree

next to the ball diamond. He and another
sixth grader had the *blue-sweater Indian*

kid in the back row of my fourth-grade photo
face down, arms spread on the ground, right

hand pinned under the blue sole of Kelly's
North Star running shoe. I didn't ask, I just

watched him crouch down and pull a shiny
black teacher's stapler from his coat pocket

and place it on the ground next to the kid's
right hand. He positioned the pointy finger,

just so, then stood, raised his right foot, and
dropped his weight on the lever, just like I do

when I staple cardboard.

—

In Grade 5, I switched to NBC, watched
CHiPs on Thursdays. When I learned Kelly

wasn't a boy, I wasn't crushed—I'd made her
a boy in my mind. I didn't bother changing it.

No one told me I had to.

Amber Alert

September 17, 2016

a little brown monkey in a tree

    random white man in a big yellow hat

brown nameless naive and alone

no breaking news
no sans serif Helvetica headline crawl
no sheriff no deputy
no police statement
no search party
no handmade posters
no handkerchiefed mama pleading your safe return
no preacher
no protest
no platinum album
no ground-breaking music video
no y-e-l-l-o-w ribbons grieving your loss

Moving Images

this is me on my bike one week after my 10th birthday
—you can barely see the Band-Aids

one week after you came home from shopping and sent me outside
to roll up the windows on the Maverick, because you said, *It looks like rain*

but there's no rain, just an old-fashioned lady's bicycle with iffy tires
and a rusted chain, propped up on a noisy kickstand, my aunt's old two-wheeler
with a shiny new purple banana seat, it smells like Grampa's barn

surprise, we're poor and I'm *the sorriest kid* on the block

because I'm crying
because I hear the names
because nasty Jackie got a new green 3 speed with rainbow streamers without asking
(and it wasn't even her birthday)
because you really wanted to surprise me
because this is what you can afford
because you really want me to love it
because I don't
because you're hugging me
because you never hug me
because you think they're tears of joy
because you're misreading all the signs
because you come outside to watch me ride
because the bike's too big and the brakes stick
because you don't seem to notice

this is me on my bike one week after my 10th birthday
leaving Alexandra Park, turning right at the hospital, flying down Alma Street
is that a cement block?

this is me, eyes locked, arms locked, chain locked flying ass over teakettle
I'm shaking under my skin, asphalt, blood, gravel, tar, I've got road all over me

this is you losing it now, right here on the front porch, in tired yellow house slippers,
denim cut-offs and your KEEP on TRUCKIN T-shirt, you look ridiculous

this is you saying ⊼く↿, ⊼く↿ *girl get your ass in the car*, grabbing your pick,
your purse, your smokes, your keys, your chequebook, and a bottle of Bactine

This is me on my bike ⊼く↿, ⊼く↿ one week after my 10th birthday
a shiny silver CCM 3 speed from Canadian Tire, black banana seat
Palmateer rookie card in my spokes
(you can barely see the Band-Aids)

Cease n Desist: From the Desk of Viola Desmond

February 14, 2012

Dear Government of Canada,

It has come to my attention that your organization has
released a postage stamp bearing my likeness for the
expressed purpose of recognizing Black History Month.
This honour comes on the heels of the official apology
and free pardon issued to me, posthumously, in 2010
by the Province of Nova Scotia. While *I* recognize the
concentrated effort to make right the past and restore
my good name, I question the methods you've employed
to place me in this position of high regard. Please *stop*

calling me the Canadian Rosa Parks. Can't a good woman
be Black *here*, without being draped in American context?
Was Jim Crow at the New Glasgow Roseland Theatre that
night? Look. Look. Just look at it. Can you see *Him* sitting
there, front and centre, in those empty seats? Selling me
that balcony ticket when I asked for the floor? Pointing
me upstairs, then calling the cops when I said *No*? Dragging
me by the arms til my skirt wrestled around my hips, til
my shoe broke loose, dangling from my ankle? Can you see
anyone offering to help me?—jailed and arrested, *before*
de Havilland pulled the knife and charged twenty dollars
for a penny crime. Tell me, *what* is there to smile about?

61 cents, I see the price of erasure. Pardon me for being
blunt, but what in Sam's simulacra were you thinking?
I went south for a reason, and not even Jim Crow could
stop me from crossing that border. Pardon me for being
tired of unravelling the myths from honourable intentions.
Your good people have a history of doing very bad things
to brown folks, so stop. Stop it. Don't flatten me with your
flattery. It's not that *I can't* appreciate the recognition—I
just don't want to. *I can* reconcile the smile for the cause,
but let's get real: I was *not* smiling that night.

So, lookit. Let this be a lesson. If our neighbours to the south
replace Andrew Jackson and put Harriet Tubman's miserable
mug on the twenty—you'd better put mine on the ten.

Veronica?

What's it like at the centre of the AGO?
Hmm. Imagine being coloured, drawn, and placed

in a wooden frame, another hung woman, positioned
just so in the middle of a landscape surrounded by rocks,

lakes, mountains, and trees, MacDonald to your right,
Carmichael to your left. Imagine being forced to look,

to spend every unblinking moment of an 8-day week
staring at a Lawren Harris landscape, a frozen wall

of whiteness, when you know, outside, the glaciers
are melting, the trees are falling, one by one,

and the Beaufort scale has shrugged and turned its
back on September. Now, the winter legends are

sold in the gift shop—T-shirts, handbags, journals, calendars,
coffee cups, board games. Puzzling, isn't it? Makes you want

to laugh, a little, knowing you've been placed *here*
by kinder hands, to reconcile the past, to challenge

the climate of the centre. I'm a sign of the times,
still, no one knows my name. *What's it like?*

It's like I'm the number one answer to the question
you haven't considered, the one you never thought

to ask, the one staring you right in the face.

Yvonne McKague Housser, Canadian, 1897–1996. Untitled, c. 1933. Oil on canvas, 66 x 50.8 cm (26 x 20 in.) Art Gallery of Ontario, Gift of Elizabeth and Tony Comper, 2011. 2011/326. © Estate of Yvonne McKague Housser.

Afterword: Aubade (Sonnet Crown)

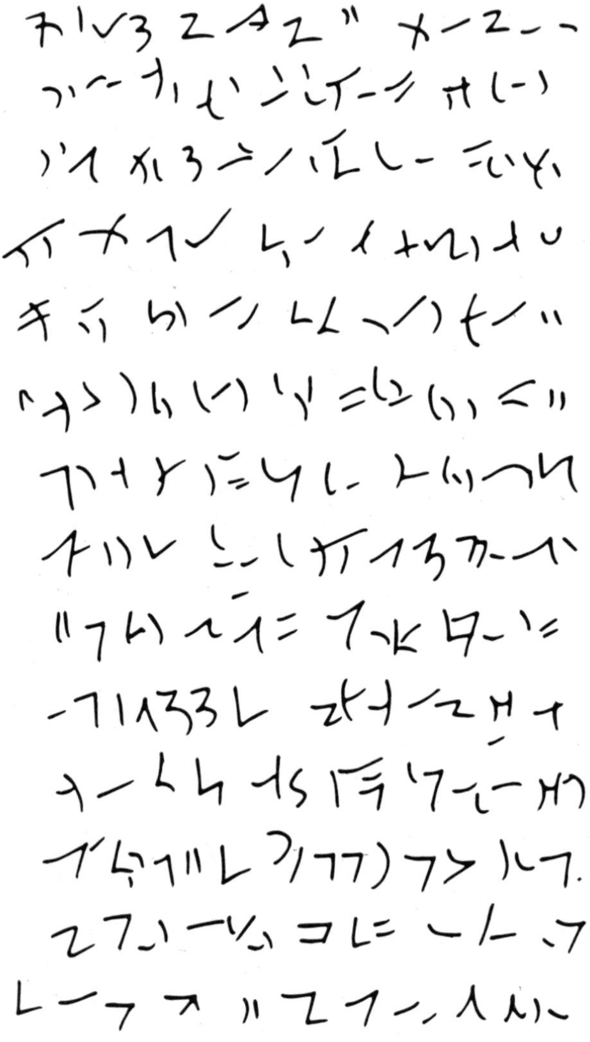

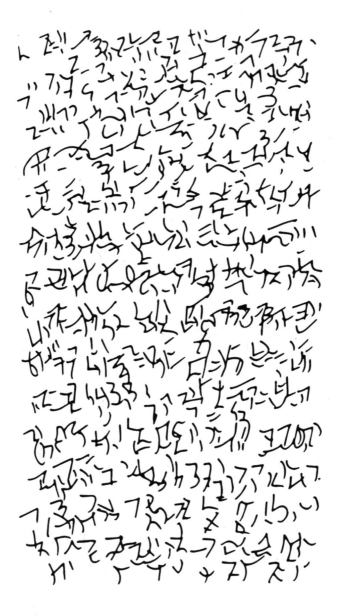

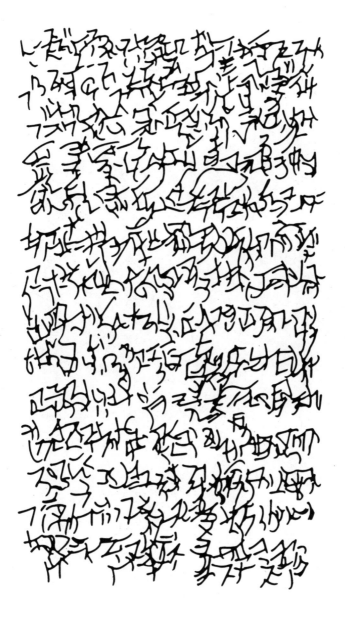

84

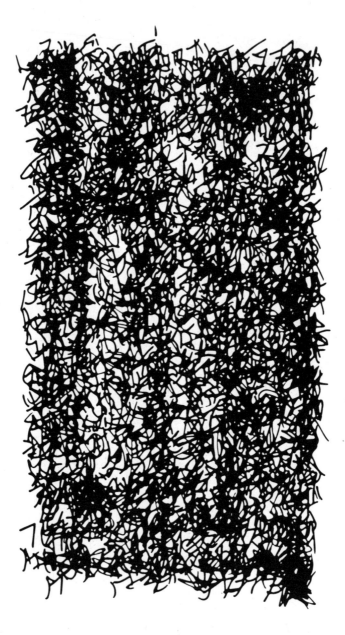

Acknowledgements

With thanks and gratitude:

To the editors of *Room magazine* and *Making Room: Forty Years of Room Magazine* for publishing "The Mountain Pine Beetle Suite."

To my editor, the brilliant Canisia Lubrin, thank you for saying yes at CWS, for your generous listening and feedback, and for encouraging me to experiment while you kept a watchful eye over the poems.

To the folks at Caitlin Press, my thanks to Vici Johnstone for getting the scoop, to Holly Vestad for your thoughtful eye, and to Michael Despotovic for your business card at a sunny, rooftop poetry reading and for thinking your former writing teacher might have something interesting to say.

To Dionne Brand and Lawrence Hill for the work and the words that inspired my critical art practice.

To distinguished authors Audre Lorde, Toni Morrison, Maya Angelou, M. NourbeSe Philip, Afua Cooper, Lorena Gale, Rita Dove, and generations of warrior writers for guiding me through this journey, and to the aggravating sisterhood of new and emerging writers who light, lift, and inspire.

To Tracy K. Smith and A. Van Jordan for teaching me how to write a poem, and to Dr. Charles Henry Rowell and the 2008 Callaloo Fellowship where several of these poems began.

To George Elliott Clarke and Wayde Compton for your pioneering work, east coast to west coast, and for your enthusiastic support of this book.

To Chelene Knight for reading my manuscript twice and for shining your light on "Centrefolds."

To Mauve Pagé, Baharak Yousefi, Hazel Plante, Kate Hennessy, Gabriela Aceves-Sepúlveda, Diane Roberts, Stephanie Dayes, Alissa Antle, and Thecla Schiphorst for your generous feedback and encouragement.

To my lil-work-bro Andrew Hawryshkewich for your dope design game.

To my family, friends, and students for your support and for showing up at my gigs.

To Joan Butterfield, my beloved mother-mentor-sister-friend, for being my witness.

Notes

How She Read is a riff on the film title *How She Move*, a 2008 hip-hop movie filmed in Toronto and directed by Ian Iqbal Rashid.

Cover image: Unknown photographer, portrait of Lorraine Gail Borden, c. 1956. Halifax, Nova Scotia. Writer's collection.

p.5: Epigraph is from Audre Lorde's poem "Call," in *Our Dead Behind Us* (New York: W. W. Norton, 1986), 73.

p.8: "Foreword" epigraph is adapted from the introduction to *The Canadian Vocabulary Speller Grade 4 Workbook* (Toronto: MacMillan Press, 1948).

p.8: Writing this book forced me to reflect on the colonizing effects of the English language and to challenge rules deeply inscribed in my thinking. This shorthand is derived from the process of deconstructing my own cursive handwriting. If you can't read it, you're not meant to.

p.12: "i've come for your demons" epigraph and selected words are from *The Pupil's Own Vocabular Speller, Grade 8, Revised Canadian Edition* (Toronto: MacMillan Press, 1947), 40.

p.13: "proper noun" epigraph is from Audre Lorde's poem "Stations," in *Our Dead Behind Us* (New York: W.W. Norton, 1986), 15.

p.14: "missing antecedents" epigraph is from Lesson 6 of *The Pupil's Own Vocabulary Speller, Grade 8, Revised Canadian Edition* (Toronto: MacMillan Press, 1947), 29.

p.21: "bullet points" epigraph is from Aurthur I. Huber, Miriam Blanton Peardon, and Celeste Comegys Gates' *We Grow Up* (London: The MacMillan Company, 1939).

p.25: "passive voice" epigraph is from Rita Dove's poem "Canary," in *Grace Notes* (New York: W.W. Norton, 1989), 64.

p.26: In "passive voice," the phrase "There's no justice—/ just us," is borrowed from the single "Devil's Pie," from D'Angelo's album *Voodoo*, released by Virgin in 2000.

p.29: In "homonyms," "Stuck on You" is from Lionel Richie's album *Can't Slow Down*, released by Motown in 1984.

p.31: In "subordinate clause," the quote "there are no honest poems / about dead women" is from Audre Lorde's poem of the same name, in *Our Dead Behind Us* (New York: W.W. Norton, 1986), 61.

p.32: Epigraph is from Dionne Brand's *Inventory* (Toronto: McClelland & Stewart, 2006), 35.

p.35: In "An Introduction to Cultural Studies," I am referencing Emanuel Jacques, a kid I didn't know, who was found murdered in Toronto in August 1977. I was ten and consumed with newspapers. Twenty years ago, I read the same stories on microfiche. Now, I Google them. There are some things you can't get over.

p.36: In "Close Reading: The Black Wench Suite," the epigraph is from Thomas McCulloch's *The Mephibosheth Stepsure Letters*, first published in the *Acadian Recorder* in 1821–23, then in paperback by McClelland & Stewart in 1960.

p.37–40: In "Close Reading: The Black Wench Suite," the quotes "From the beginning...," "What was the narrative moment...," and "what weighty price..." are from Toni Morrison's *Playing in the Dark: Whiteness and the Literary Imagination* (New York: Vintage, 1993).

p.41: "'Nuff Said" pays homage to "Ain't Got No, I Got Life" from Nina Simone's album *'Nuff Said*, released by RCA Victor in 1968.

p.43: "Don't Call Me Minty" epigraph is quoted from the introduction to Harriet Tubman on the Historica Canada website.

p.43: In "Don't Call Me Minty," Tubman's illness and diagnosis are taken from Kate Clifford Larson's *Bound for the Promised Land: Harriet Tubman: Portrait of an American Hero* (New York: Ballantine Books, 2004), 42.

p.45: "Centrefolds" epigraph is from Dionne Brand's poem "Blues Spiritual for Mammy Prater," in *No Language is Neutral* (Toronto: Coach House, 1990), 16.

p.46–47: The photograph of Delia is one of fifteen remaining photographs taken by Joseph T. Zealy in 1850, commissioned by zoologist Louis Agassiz. "Marie-Thérèse" is the name of the sitter in the portrait by François Malépart de Beaucourt, doubly objectified, both de Beaucourt's slave and his subject. I met these women while co-writing a paper about Harriet Tubman, with Monique Silverman for *Canadian Art Review* in 2005. I couldn't let them go, couldn't stop them from talking.

p.53: "Excerpts" epigraph is from the play *Angélique* by Lorena Gale (Toronto: Playwrights Canada, 1999).

p.53–55: In "Excerpts," "sister scholars" and the "aggravating sisterhood" honours those who have recovered Angélique. Notably, playwright Lorena Gale wrote *Angélique*, which was staged in 1995, and Dr. Afua Cooper, writer, historian, and poet, wrote *The Hanging of Angélique: The Untold Story of Canadian Slavery and the Burning of Old Montreal* (New York: HarperCollins, 2006). More recently, Carlton University students Natalie Berchem, Allison Smith, and Jessica Walkden produced *Marie-Joseph Angélique: Trial of a Rebel Slave*, a historical short documentary in 2013.

p.56: *Sad Young Black Girl Perched on Bench* is an image from "Free Black North," a photography exhibit at the Art Gallery of Ontario featuring the descendants of Black refugees from the US living in Ontario in the mid-1800s. It ran from April–October 2017.

p.63: The term *punctum* is from Roland Barthes' *Camera Lucida* (New York: Hill & Wang, 1980). I know it as a detail in a photo, image, or sign that triggers a thought, a memory which propels the viewer beyond the fact of the image.

p.64: "The Tiny People" epigraph is from a letter by Mary Livingstone in M. NourbeSe Philip's *Looking for Livingstone: An Odyssey of Silence* (St. Andrews: Mercury Press, 1991).

p.64–65: "The Tiny People" is adapted from *The Canadian Vocabulary Speller Grade 4 Workbook* (Toronto: MacMillan Press, 1948). The story "The Tiny People" is adapted from Lesson 20 on page 39.

p.66: "Editorial" epigraph is from Jane Rhodes' *Mary Ann Shadd Cary: The Black Press and Protest in the Nineteenth Century* (Bloomington: Indiana University Press, 1999). Shadd's original address was originally published in *The Provincial Freeman*, October 21, 1854.

p.68: In "Mixed Bowling," *The Garden of Earthly Delights* is a tryptic by Dutch painter Hieronymus Bosch. It dates 1490–1510.

p.72: "Simcoe Days:" Lieutenant-Governor John Graves Simcoe didn't stop slavery, but, to his credit, he brokered the Act to Limit Slavery in Upper Canada, July 9, 1793. Too late for Chloe Cooley. Both are remembered in Ontario with commemorative plaques.

p.75: "Amber Alert:" According to curiousgeorge.com, September 16, 2017 is Curiosity Day. "This initiative celebrates the magic of learning and discovery through reading as only George and The Man in the Yellow Hat can." Like I said, there are some things you just can't get over.

p.77: "Cease n Desist:" The Viola Desmond postage stamp was issued February 1, 2012. According to canadianpostagestamps.ca, "The strong and flattering portrait provides a central focus, and silhouettes of significant places appear at the bottom. This stamp is intended to have a historical look and feel, as well as a richness and human warmth." This is the double-ness of the stamp, making history visible while erasing it at the same time.

According to www.bloomberg.com, US agencies have been instructed to halt the production of the Harriet Tubman twenty-dollar bill. Her image was to replace confederate leader and slave holder Andrew Jackson. In light of Charlottesville, Virginia, and the current racial climate in the US under President Donald Trump, the project has been delayed until 2026.

Viola Desmond will be the new face on the Canadian ten-dollar bill in 2018.

p.78: "Veronica?": According to the caption next to "Untitled [Veronica?]," a pencil notation on the back of the canvas reads *Veronica*. This may be Veronica MacLeod, an art model employed by the gallery in the 1930s and 1940s.

Photo Dale Northey

Author bio

Chantal Gibson is an artist-educator interested in the cultural production of knowledge. Her work explores the overlap between literary and visual art and challenges imperialist notions quietly embedded in everyday things—from academic school books to kitschy souvenir spoons. An award-winning instructor, she teaches in the School of Interactive Arts & Technology at Simon Fraser University. chantalgibson.com

This book is set in Arno Pro, designed by Robert Slimbach.
The text was typeset by Vici Johnstone.

Caitlin Press, Spring 2019.